#RisingLeader
Dr. Neva Helena Alexander

I0484238

Contents

Preface

This book was created for youth who aspire to lead or improve their leadership skills in their communities, schools, universities, or workplaces. The aim of the author is for young people to become leaders in the many aspects of their lives. This book will help you understand the concept of 'born leader", decision making, group and team effectiveness, the dynamics of working in the community as well as how to lead with passion, how to be a critical thinker and how to represent values to people. Case studies are presented to help readers better understand these principles. This book will give you an improved perspective on leadership.

To get the most value from this book which aims to develop your leadership knowledge and skills, you should engage in the various activities found in each chapter. These activities are designed to increase your understanding of your strengths and weaknesses as a leader. They also provide you with approaches to expanding your proficiency as a leader. Ideally, your leadership abilities should continue to improve as you gain knowledge about yourself and the techniques you can use to motivate and inspire others to achieve a common goal.

Chapter 1: Born As a Leader?

"The most dangerous leadership myth is that leaders are born — that there is a genetic factor to leadership. That's nonsense; in fact, the opposite is true. Leaders are made rather than born."

— Warren Bennis

Are leaders born or made? That is, can your genes make a difference to your career? This is one of the oldest questions associated with leadership. As the saying goes by William Shakespeare in his play *Twelfth Night*, "some are born great, some achieve greatness, and some have greatness thrust upon them."

A study in 2013 by a leading military academy claimed to have proven the theory that great leaders such as Sir Winston Churchill or Margaret Thatcher are all born and not made. The study was published in the American Psychological Association's *Journal of Applied Psychology*. The officers, eighty-seven of whom were men, were defined as being more psychologically complex if they had a more diverse sense of their own abilities as leaders. In addition to a series of questions and physical and mental tests, half underwent what is called "brain mapping". Using electrodes placed on nineteen different locations on the officers' heads, researchers were able to track activity in particular areas of the brain while the officers were at rest.

Researchers also tested leadership and decision-making abilities using hypnosis. The participating officers had to lead their unit to interact with hostile and non-hostile civilians, enemy forces and the media. They eventually had to lead the mission of shooting down a US helicopter during an international humanitarian relief mission in Africa. Former military officers with significant experience in these types of situations rated the officers' responses to the scenario based on them being able to adapt, being aware, and making good decisions. Officers who had a more complex sense of their leadership skills were found to be more adaptable and effective leaders. As such, it is believed they were born leaders.

On the other hand, you will find many individuals who believe that leaders are made. The slogans of some top organizations state that they can make you a leader. I believe that leadership potential exists within each of us. That potential can be sparked by outside events, or it can be discovered by exploring ourselves from within. Once you learn the techniques of true leadership, you will be able to gain the confidence it takes to become a leader. A current example of such a leader would be Malala Yousufzai, who became known to the world after surviving an assassination attempt by the Taliban. She decided to take a stand against terrorism and against the oppression towards education.

The mark of a true leader is not necessarily determined by a position or title held, but by how many people are willing to follow you. As long as there have been leaders, there have been those who tried to determine how and why they were successful. Leadership itself has not changed, but our understanding of it has. It is important to understand why different leadership styles can be effective, why the same leadership style will not work in every situation, and which leadership style best fits your personality or communication style. Everyone has leadership potential within him/her, but understanding these concepts will help you maximize your leadership skill.

Defining Leadership

"Control is not leadership; management is not leadership; leadership is leadership. If you seek to lead, invest at least 50% percent of your time in leading yourself—your own purpose, ethics, principles, motivation, conduct. Invest at least 20% percent leading those with authority over you and 15% percent leading your peers."
— Dee Hock
Founder and former CEO Emeritus, Visa

Would you like to be a lawyer, health professional, teacher, entertainer, or owner of your own business? Well, a great part of any career involves leadership. Leadership is not only for those who seek to partake in a "leadership position," but also for those who will work with leaders. For one to be successful in life, one must have leadership skills. But do you understand leadership?

Everyone has some understanding of the concept of leadership, because he/she has experienced situations where he/she at least has been a follower—if not a leader. People also have ideas — based on their cultural customs and past experiences as followers—about the way leaders should behave. Yet, developing a single definition of leadership has been hard to achieve, because leadership is a complex concept influenced by many variables. Some of the variables affecting leadership include: the personal characteristics of the leader, the expectations and backgrounds of the followers, and the type of environment or organization in which the individual attempts to lead others. As a result, the varied definitions address only some of the many facets or variables affecting the interaction between leaders and followers.

The general model of leadership supports an individual who acts as a leader and one or more individuals who act as followers. The leader interacts with the followers to ultimately motivate them to perform the actions desired by the leader. Effective leadership is then evident when the group achieves a goal set by the leader or displays behaviors that the leader considers to be acceptable. The general leadership model, however, does not explain how the leader motivates others or why the followers accept the goals promoted by the leader and take the actions necessary to achieve the goals.

Leadership among Youth

Youth leadership is the practice of teenagers and young adults exercising authority over themselves or others. Many programs around the world seek to teach young people particular skills associated with leadership. The concept of youth leadership was also examined with the goal of identifying a working definition. Some definitions of youth leadership refer to it as the ability to lead others or get others to work together toward a common goal or vision. More often than not, definitions of youth leadership focus on the ability to lead yourself and work with others. Youth should have the ability to evaluate their strengths and weaknesses, set personal and vocational goals, and have self-esteem.

Leaders Then and Now

Successful young leaders are not new to this generation. History is rife with notable young leaders who have helped build the early foundations of youth leadership.

Be the kind of leader that you would follow.

Youth Leaders in History

In this section you will find young leaders that made a great impact in history. These leaders may or may not be the best, but they had followers and were able to achieve their goals.

Imperator Caesar Divi Filius Augustus

Augustus was born in 63 B.C. as the son of Gaius Octavius. In his early teens, he was sent to Apollonia, a city in modern-day Albania. He was 18 years old when he heard the news of Julius Caesar's assassination. Caesar had no legitimate children so he left Augustus two-thirds of his estate and named him both his son and heir. Set on following in his adopted father's footsteps, Augustus began to gather support of those loyal to Caesar by emphasizing his status as the rightful heir to Caesar.

On May 6, 44 B.C., 18-year-old Augustus led an army of more than 3,000 veteran troops into Rome. He did not have a lot of resistance since many were compassionate to his cause.

He succeeded in driving Caesar's assassins out of the city. With the Senate's attitude towards Antony shifting from friend to enemy, Augustus began to build his military forces, even winning over two of Antony's legions with the promise of higher wages. Augustus was inaugurated to the Senate at the tender age of 19, and eventually become the first emperor of the Roman Empire. He died in 14 A.D. at the age of 75.

Alexander the Great

Alexander was born in 356 B.C. as the son of the Macedonian king, Philip II. When he was 13 years old, he was sent to Mieza to be taught by Aristotle. He had classmates such as Ptolemy, Hephaistion, and Cassander. When he was 16, he returned to Macedon to rule as regent while his father waged war against Byzantium. It was during this time that Alexander saw his first military action by leading a small force against the Thracian Maedi. The Maedi greatly underestimated the powers of Alexander which caused him to be driven from the area. This would be the first of many victories for Alexander. When he was 17, his father placed him as the head of a small army, sending him to conquer revolts in southern Thrace, which he did with ease. By the time of his death at age 32, he had conquered most of the ancient world. He is regarded by many today as the greatest military commander of all time.

Cleopatra

Cleopatra is said to be the most beautiful woman in the history of the human race, who successfully ruled the hearts of the most powerful men of that time. Her beauty has been a subject of discussion and an inspiration for art in popular Western culture. On the other hand, according to many historians, Cleopatra was described as masculine-looking with thin lips, prominent chin and a long, hooked nose. This, they say, has been backed by images of the Queen that have been unearthed through the statues and coins of that era. However, beautiful or not, it is believed that she was definitely the most tactful and intelligent leader of her time. Smart, powerful and authoritative, she acquired the throne at the tender age of 18, following the death of her father and she remained the ruler until her death. She married two of her brothers and was involved in the murder of two of her siblings, one brother and one sister, to safeguard the throne for herself and her son, Caesarion. In a male-dominated society, Cleopatra not only managed to hold the country together but served as a powerful leader as any of her male colleagues.

William Pitt

William Pitt the Younger (28 May 1759 – 23 January 1806) was a British politician of the late 18th and early 19th centuries. He became the youngest Prime Minister in 1783 at the age of 24. He left office in 1801, but was Prime Minister again from 1804 until his death in 1806. He was also the Chancellor of the Exchequer throughout his premiership. He is known as "the Younger" to distinguish him from his father, William Pitt the Elder, who had previously served as Prime Minister.

The younger Pitt's prime ministerial tenure, which came during the reign of George III, was dominated by major events in Europe, including the French Revolution and the Napoleonic Wars. Pitt, although often referred to as a Tory, or "new Tory", called himself an "independent Whig" and was generally opposed to the development of a strict partisan political system.

Young Leaders of Today

"I told myself, Malala, you have already faced death. This is your second life. Don't be afraid if you are afraid, you can't move forward." – Malala Yousafzai

Malala Yousafzai

At the age of 11, Yousafzai was writing under a pseudonym for the BBC, detailing what it's like to live under Taliban rule. In 2009, The New York Times filmed a documentary about her life. Yousafzai is an influential communicator and education activist. In October 2012, she was shot in the back of the head by Taliban gunmen, but survived the assassination attempt. Yousafzai was the recipient of the UN 2013 Human Rights Prize and is the youngest person to have ever received a Nobel Prize.

Saran Kaba Jones

Saran Kaba Jones is the founder of FACE Africa, a group working to provide access to clean drinking water for thousands of people in rural parts of Liberia. Since its launch in 2009, FACE Africa has implemented several water and sanitation projects in under-served communities in the country, including building hand-dug wells, rehabilitating existing wells and constructing communal latrines.

Jared Cohen

Jared Cohen is the founder and director of Google Ideas and an advisor to the executive chairman at Google, Inc. He is also an adjunct senior fellow at the Council on Foreign Relations and a bestselling author. Previously he served as a member of the Secretary of State's Policy Planning Staff and as a close advisor to both Condoleezza Rice and Hillary Clinton.

Steps You Can Take to Become a Successful Young Leader
The reality is that you might not be a star overnight but you can start preparing yourself for what the future might offer.

1) *Start preparing before and after you enter the workforce.*

   Volunteer in social or nonprofit organizations or clubs

   where you can develop or improve your leadership skills.

2) *Do your homework.* Most of what you'll need to be a good

   leader you'll learn through experience, but it is important

   to read books or take professional development courses on

   leadership so that you can develop your leadership skills.

3) *Take time to assess the culture of the organization.* If you are

   doing an internship or working full time, listen to and

   observe how staff members treat new workers and learn

   what their expectations are.

4) *Identify areas where you can provide new insight or help.* There

   is always room for improvement.

5) *Offer your help.* Offering help is not giving away your time

   for free. Offering builds relationships and can open

   opportunities for you.

6) *Network.* You can network in the community, at the

university, at work, and through professional

organizations. By networking you can establish

relationships and find a mentor to assist with your

development.

Leadership Qualities

You will usually find certain qualities in leaders. These qualities can be taught so that you can be made into a leader. Following are some key qualities that every good leader should possess and learn to emphasize.

Honesty: It makes people feel like they know where they stand with you at all times. Good leaders are extremely ethical and believe that honesty, effort, and reliability form the foundation of success.

Communicate: Knowing what you want accomplished may seem clear in your head, but if you try to explain it to someone else and are met with a blank look, you know there is a problem. Being able to clearly describe what you want done is very important.

Confidence: If you don't believe in yourself, no one will. Not only are the best leaders confident, but their confidence is infectious. People are naturally drawn to them, seek their advice, and feel more confident as a result.

Creativity: As a leader, it's important to learn to think outside the box.

Inspire: Leaders challenge their people by setting high but realistic goals and expectations. They give them the support, tools, training, and latitude to pursue those goals and become the best they can possibly be.

Focus: Know where you're going. Extraordinary leaders plan ahead and they are extremely organized.

Passion: You must have passion for what you're doing. Live, breathe, eat, and sleep your mission.

Care: Effective leaders do not just care about themselves, but about others.

Integrity: Leaders are people who are respected and worth listening to.

Empowering: True leaders make their associates feel encouraged and powerful, not useless and powerless.

Self-awareness: You need to be clear on what your strengths are and what complementary strengths you need from others.

What Makes a Leader Popular?

What do all popular people have in common? For one they are confident, they socialize, they take risks, they stay in the spotlight, and they give back to their community. Leaders don't hide in the corner. They get up and put themselves in the spotlight. They don't worry about how they look or what other people think about them. Popular leaders put themselves out there. This means they step out of their comfort zone. If you want to be likable try the following: making conversation, cracking jokes, flirting, and in general, engaging people. Remember that popular people are popular only because they are known and get attention from others. To be popular, you're going to need to take a few chances on a social level that may normally feel uncomfortable to you. So be prepared to be bold. Popular people are on friendly terms with pretty much everyone--not only their peers, but also the teachers, the supervisors, the grocery store clerk, the janitor, the parents, the kids, and generally anyone who's even the tiniest bit nice. They're on good enough terms that they can hold a short, friendly conversation with anyone in the room. There's no reason you can't do that, too. Being friendly doesn't take a big effort, but it makes a real impact.

Summary
People have different points of view on whether leaders are born or made. You can improve your leadership skills by understanding the qualities of a good leader. Additionally, you can take the time to attend development leadership classes, be active in your community, network, build relationships, and find a mentor.

Case Study 1: The Job Interview
HSBC is a multinational bank headquartered in London, with operations in eighty-six countries. The firm uses a team approach to the management of relationships with customers at the HSBC Private Bank business unit. The business unit provides financial services ranging from managing brokerage to purchasing gems and precious metals on behalf of high-net-worth clients. The bank is currently conducting interviews to fill a vacancy for the position of senior director (Middle East).

Amirah, a ten-year veteran of the division, working in the London headquarters, is applying for the position and will be interviewed by several senior managers who are all males. She is confident that she has the technical skills for the position but is concerned that she may not have enough experience as a leader. Amirah anticipates that the interviewers will ask her questions about leadership — particularly her definition of leadership. To prepare for the interview, she is reviewing some of the numerous and varied definitions of leadership. Each definition seems to emphasize something different, like: the personality traits of the leader or the quality of the relationships between the leader and the follower. To increase her confusion, she cannot decide if the senior managers in the private banking division value reaching corporate goals more than developing an empowered and cooperative team. At the same time, she knows that any definition of leadership that she gives will have to be concise.

Questions:
1.   What are the elements of leadership that Amirah should consider as basic to the definition of leadership?
2.   What definition of leadership should Amirah give during the interview?
3.   How does this definition of leadership apply to the specific situation of the team approach in HSBC Private Bank?

Chapter 2: Understanding Yourself
"What I am looking for is not out there; it is in me."

— Helen Keller

Good leaders understand themselves. As a leader, you need to know your capabilities. What can you do? What are your strengths? What are your weaknesses? Will your weaknesses hinder your ability to be a good leader, or will your strengths help you to excel beyond your potential?

I once taught a student — I will call her Cindy — who aspired to be student president. Cindy did well in all her classes. She was well mannered but lacked self-confidence. One day Cindy came to my office to express her aspirations. I quickly realized that because of her lack of self-confidence she did not have many friends, and by not having friends she would have a difficult time winning the student election. Additionally, I realized that Cindy did not know her abilities.

The first step in developing skills and abilities is to "understand you" .The importance of self-knowledge for leadership may seem obvious. Nonetheless, many leaders do not have enough knowledge about their behaviors and the way they interact with others. Personal preferences for certain types of behaviors can also result in leaders using the same leadership style and methods regardless of the situation. Increasing self-knowledge and self-understanding can improve your ability to interact with others, which is important in effective leadership.

Self-understanding is related to emotional intelligence. This means that people have different abilities to manage themselves and their relationships with others. To manage yourself, you must have a relatively high degree of self-awareness, which includes knowledge about yourself, such as your personal preferences and reactions to different situations. You also have to be aware of how you interact with others — particularly in stressful situations where you may be emotionally upset. Self-understanding can be improved by reflection and objective analysis of your strengths and weaknesses, which Cindy had to work on.

Identifying Your Strengths and Weaknesses

Everyone has strengths and weaknesses with respect to leadership. The strengths are personal attributes that can be useful for developing and exercising leadership skills. For example, you may be comfortable talking to strangers, or you may have more knowledge about a particular topic than others. The weaknesses are factors that can hamper your ability to develop and exercise leadership skills. Weaknesses can include difficulties with trusting others and poor attention to detail. You can think of strength as any trait or characteristic that will help you become an effective leader and a weakness as any trait or characteristic that will interfere with leadership.

Identifying your strengths and weaknesses may be difficult, because it requires objective self-assessment. It is important for leadership, because you want to emphasize your strengths when faced with a leadership task. At the same time, you should be continuously working on improving your weaknesses to ensure that they do not hamper your future leadership efforts.

One approach to identifying your leadership strengths and weaknesses is to write a reflective essay about a leadership experience. The experience does not have to involve a formal leadership position and can focus on a time when you influenced others to strive toward a goal that you proposed. By describing the situation and interaction, you can evaluate your behaviors and feelings that can be considered strengths or weaknesses. To be effective, you must be honest in your evaluation.

Another approach to identifying strengths and weaknesses is to think about the traits or characteristics that you have observed in others who are in positions of leadership and assess whether you have these traits or characteristics. Observing others can help you understand the way that some personality characteristics — such as sociability or imagination — are valuable for leadership. Observing others may also reveal some of the traits associated with poor leadership that can be considered weaknesses, such as arrogance or lacking concern for others. Comparing yourself with other leaders can create standards for personal appraisal of your own strengths and weaknesses.

Take the time to ask others about your strengths and weaknesses as a leader. You can also use social media such as Facebook and Twitter to get comments on your strengths and weaknesses. You may be surprised by what they tell you. They may identify some characteristics or behaviors as strengths that you did not think were important for leadership. If they are honest with their reviews, they also may reveal some weaknesses that you may not have considered. The information that others provide can increase your understanding of leadership abilities, because it tells you how others see you.

Discovering Your Leadership Strengths and Weaknesses

How you react naturally to a situation can tell you about your leadership strengths and weaknesses. Consider how you would initially react in each of the following situations that require some type of action. Add up your total score to help you identify some of your strengths and weaknesses.

				Score
1. Think of a challenging situation you have experienced that involved danger, such as a child running in front of an oncoming automobile. How did you react?	Withdrew 1	Observed 2	Intervened 3	
2. How do you act when you enter a room crowded with other women/men?	Find a quiet corner to talk with one person 1	Watch others until an opportunity arises to join a conversation 2	Attempt to talk with as many people as possible 3	
3. How do you react in a situation where you do not	Wait and see what will happen	Try to collect as much information as possible	Take an action, if necessary, based on the	

understand what is happening?	1	2	information I have 3	
4. How do you react when someone else does not understand what is happening?	Let them find out what is happening on their own 1	Help them find out what is happening 2	Tell them what is happening 3	
5. How do you react when someone else proposes a new idea?	Let the person provide you with more information 1	Work with the other person to find more information 2	Explore the new idea on your own 3	

To gain some insight into your leadership strengths and weaknesses, add up the scores and compare your total to the following chart.

Score	Strengths	Weaknesses
5–8	Willingness to delegate responsibility to others; willingness to help others develop their leadership skills	Slow to take action to change conditions in your environment; may have difficulty networking with others because of a tendency to be introverted; a tendency to avoid

		intervening in a situation—even if it is necessary
9–12	Ability to work with others to solve problems; ability to collect and analyze information before making a leadership decision; value consensus before action on a problem or situation	Difficulty making a rapid decision when there is insufficient information; difficulty changing leadership approaches based on the situation
13–15	Willingness to act decisively to make positive changes in the environment; ability to establish networks with other people	Difficulty in working with others and delegating responsibility; difficulty with accepting input from others; tendency to excessively direct others

What is Your Passion?

Cindy was very passionate to lead her peers. Because of this passion she was making the steps to understand herself. Passion is an overwhelming feeling of attraction for something or someone that is an emotional response not based on reason. People can be passionate about a hobby or their work. They can be passionate about an idea or a social movement. They can be passionate about other people in their lives. When people feel passion, they are no longer indifferent about something or someone in their lives.

Passion is a key factor for leadership. Effective leaders are passionate about achieving a goal or objective; passion increases their commitment. Passionate people are more dedicated because of their strong desire to reach a goal. Passion functions as a personal motivator for leaders, encouraging them to take the specific actions necessary to achieve a goal. It contributes to developing the enthusiasm and confidence necessary to lead others.

Only you can decide what you feel passionate about. It may be a cause, a job, or relationships with your family. You may already know what you feel passionate about based on your interests and experiences. Because passion is an emotion, it is difficult to contain or control once it is lit. When you become involved with something you feel passionate about, it is easier to remain focused and inspired. Your passions also reflect your values and implicitly communicate these values to others. For example, if you are passionate about improving social conditions, others perceive that you are dedicated to helping people.

Despite the importance of passion in leadership, it can be harmful if the passion grows into an obsession to achieve a goal or objective, which occurs when a person becomes excessively focused on achieving a goal with all energy directed to a single purpose.

You can make your passion influence your ability to lead others. As a result, you should recognize the things you feel most passionate about and understand the degree of emotion you feel. At the same time, you should understand that passions tend to change over time. What you feel passionate about today may not be what you feel passionate about in years ahead. As a result, you should continually consider whether you still feel passionate about the same things or people as you have in the past. This will improve your understanding of your passions and their usefulness in leadership.

Identifying Your Leadership Style

"Leadership style" is the term used to describe the way a leader interacts with followers to attempt to influence behaviors. To be effective leaders, all individuals must develop a leadership style that is suitable for their personality. Your leadership style will generally be consistent over time, because it is the approach you are most comfortable with. At the same time, you have to be aware that your natural leadership styles may not be suitable in all situations. A person's leadership style can have a strong influence on followers and their motivation to pursue the goals that the leader establishes. As a result, the best leadership style for you may be a flexible blend of different styles that you use in different situations.

There are three basic leadership styles: autocratic, participative, and laissez-faire also known as free-rein styles. These three styles can be visualized on a scale, with autocratic on one end, laissez-faire on the other end, and participative in the middle. Leaders are positioned at different points on the scale based on their preferences of elements from the different leadership styles. At the same time, they can knowingly adjust their style to change their position on the scale based on the needs of followers and the specific situation. Figure 1 shows the scale of leadership styles ranging from authoritative to laissez-faire.

Autocratic leaders- Autocratic leaders are highly directive and provide followers with precise instructions about the way tasks should be performed. They also do not generally accept advice from followers about alternate approaches to solving the problems or performing the tasks necessary to achieve a goal. The relationship between the autocratic leader and the follower is characterized by information flowing in only one direction. Autocratic leaders tend to stand apart from followers, believing that distance is necessary to maintain their authority. Many organizations discourage leaders from using the autocratic style, because it is associated with excessively controlling or dictatorial behaviors.

Even though autocratic leadership may not be widely encouraged, it is still in practice. It is said that autocratic leaders (a) make plans independent of followers, (b) do not explain their actions, (c) refuse to compromise, (d) do not maintain a friendly relationship with followers, and (e) discourage followers' use of questions for obtaining information.

Participative leadership-In the participative leadership style, the leader allows all members of a group of followers to participate in the decision-making process, which can include allowing the members of the group to vote for a specific alternative. The leader of the group encourages others to participate in the decision-making process, based on the belief that the followers will more readily accept the outcome if they are involved in the decision-making process. The participative leadership style encompasses the consensual leader who requires all followers to agree to a decision and a consultative leader who asks followers about their opinions but retains full decision-making authority. The consultative leader is the most common type of participative leader, because the leader ultimately remains responsible for outcomes in most organizations.

Laissez-faire leadership- Leaders who use the laissez-faire style of leadership assign a goal to followers who are then responsible for determining how the goal will be achieved. The leader does not become involved unless the followers ask for assistance or advice. This leadership style requires the leader to have a high level of trust in followers. It also requires the leader to provide clear expectations about the goal and the boundaries for the activities that the employees can use to achieve the goal.

Each leadership style is suitable for different types of circumstances. The authoritarian style is effective if there is very little time for the group to make a decision or if the leader has more knowledge about the problem than the various members of the group. The participative style of leadership is effective with followers from individualistic cultures who expect some degree of input into the leader's decision-making process. It is also useful in increasing the perception of employees that they have a greater amount of control over their work environment, which may be useful for motivating assembly-line workers. The laissez-faire leadership style can be effective if the followers are experts in a field and can easily determine how to achieve a goal without any formal guidance from a leader. An example of a situation in which the laissez-faire style could be appropriate is with a group of researchers attempting to develop an innovative product.

Understanding your leadership style requires that you determine where you fit on the autocratic–participative–laissez-faire scale. Ask yourself how comfortable you are with letting others make most of the decisions. You should also consider whether you focus on tasks or on relationships with others. Gaining a better understanding of your natural leadership style can help you use that style when appropriate and shift toward using other styles when required by the situation.

The day Cindy left my office she realized she had a lot of work to do in order for her to win the student election. Cindy decided not to run for office until she followed the steps I gave her to understanding herself. The following year she ran for vice-president and won.

Summary

Self-understanding is important for effective leadership. You have to understand your leadership strengths to emphasize these characteristics when leading others. You also have to recognize your leadership weaknesses to help you understand the way these weaknesses can interfere with effective leadership. An effective leader is also passionate, communicating excitement and enthusiasm to followers. Understanding your preferred leadership style is important to develop the skills required to alter your style, when necessary, in a specific situation. One approach to understanding leadership style is to consider whether you tend to be an autocratic, participative, or laissez-faire leader. Another approach to understanding leadership style is to determine if you are a task-oriented or relationship-oriented leader. Effective leaders are responsible for making decisions—regardless of their leadership style. The use of a structured framework to the decision-making process can help leaders make better decisions.

Case Study 2: The Manager's Leadership Style

Jessica is the manager of an ambulatory care unit at a hospital and is directly responsible for a staff of twenty-five physicians, nurses, and technicians. She considers herself a good leader, because she meets the goals set by the senior managers of the hospital and rarely receives complaints from staff. She believes that her success as a leader is because she focuses on details and on making sure that all work is performed on time and with the highest quality.
She also believes that the hospital is providing an important service for the community and is proud to be in charge of the ambulatory care unit.

The unit has a high staff turnover when compared to other units, but Jessica believes that this is not a significant problem. Several of the departing staff members have told her they are leaving because they want more autonomy when making professional decisions. Jessica considers the desire for greater autonomy among staff unrealistic, because employees cannot be trusted to perform tasks correctly without close supervision. If they make a mistake, it will affect the quality of patient treatment and reflect badly on Jessica. During these exit interviews, she is often uncomfortable discussing these matters with staff, but she forces herself to pay attention because it is a requirement of her position.

Questions:

1. What are some of Jessica's strengths and weaknesses?
2. Where would you position Jessica on the autocratic–participative–laissez-faire continuum of leadership style?
3. Does Jessica have a task-oriented or relationship-oriented leadership style? Why?
4. How can Jessica improve her decision making?

Chapter 3: Lead with Passion

"Without passion you don't have energy; without energy you have nothing."
                                                    —Donald Trump

The previous chapter discussed the importance of passion for effective leadership. To lead others, you must feel passionate about what you are doing. The enthusiasm and commitment you feel can be your personal strengths to help you become an effective leader, because inspiring others becomes a natural extension of the way you feel about the goal or objective you are working to achieve.

Passion is infectious. When you feel passionate about something, you automatically communicate your feelings authentically and convincingly to others. Your passion pulls you toward your goals and motivates you to pull others along with you. A leader who is passionate can more easily inspire others to become passionate about achieving the goals. In contrast, people are reluctant to follow a leader who does not demonstrate a strong passion to achieve a vision for the future of the group or organization.

Profiled below are some leaders who despite all odds remained passionate about what they believe in.

Mother Teresa: This quiet, petite, and humble woman spent fifty years working among the poorest people in 133 countries. She described her mission as giving "Wholehearted and Free service to the poorest of the poor." She was passionate about helping the poor.

Henry Ford: Despite business failure (the Ford Motor Company was actually his third attempt to start an automobile-manufacturing company) and others' dismissal of his ideas, he never gave up. He was passionate about automobiles.

Mohandas Karamchand Gandhi: He was the preeminent leader of Indian nationalism in British-ruled India. Employing nonviolent civil disobedience, Gandhi led India to independence and inspired movements for civil rights and freedom across the world. He was passionate about independence. Similar to Martin Luther King Jr., another passionate leader, he wanted to bring black and white people together.

Nelson Mandela: He was the first South African president elected in fully democratic elections. Mandela was also the main player in the anti-apartheid movements in the country and served a lengthy prison sentence because of the same. Can you state the name of four other leaders who were passionate?

1) _____

2) _____

3) _____

4) _____

Finding Your Passion

When you feel passionate, you are energized and motivated to take action to use your passion to achieve a purpose. Finding your passion will help you become a leader, because it will help you communicate your excitement to others, which can inspire them to pursue goals and objectives related to your passion. It will also help you recognize that you have a purpose that is related to your passions.

Finding your passion may be difficult. There may be many things you like to do—but only a few things that make you feel passionate. The following exercises are to help you identify the things that matter most to you. While the activities may seem simple, they require you to think carefully regarding the way you feel about the way you can affect the world around you.

Exercise 1: Passion in Your Daily Life

Pay attention to the things that excite you as you go about the tasks of your daily life. You may find a subject in school or information that you hear from others in the community to be exciting. You may also find that various ideas or groups create a desire to help achieve a common goal. Over the next few days, prepare a list of ten things that excite you. Also, rate the degree of excitement you feel about the subject, ranging from "1" for mildly excited to "5" for extremely excited. When the list is complete, you should be able to identify the two or three things that create the greatest amount of passion for you.

	What Excites Me	Score 1–5
1.		
2.		
3.		

4. _____

5. _____

6. _____

7. _____

8. _____

9. _____

10. _____

Exercise 2: Road Map to a Passionate Future

After you identify the things about which you feel most passionate, you should begin thinking about how you can make your passions into a reality. You have to use reasoning and common sense in this process. However, it may not be possible to do everything you feel passionate about—at least right away. Some things need careful planning and preparation. For example, if you are passionate about helping others, you may have to take specific educational programs to learn the necessary skills. To help you map the way to a passionate future, you should keep a journal in which you write down the many different approaches you can take to do the things about which you feel passionate.

The journal entries should focus on a major goal related to something you feel passionate about. You should also be able to break the major goal into several subgoals. For each subgoal, list the different things that will help you achieve your subgoal. This can help you create a road map leading to the future when you will be involved with the things you feel most passionate about. Following is an example of how you can use a journal to practise logic and common sense in assisting you to achieve goals related to your passions.

Goal: To teach literacy to adults who cannot read or write

Subgoal: 1) To help illiterate women to learn how to read and write
> Steps to Achieve Goal:
> a) Obtain training in teaching reading and writing
> b) Obtain training in adult education

Subgoal: 2) To establish a literacy program in my community
> Steps to Achieve Goal:
> a) Obtain experience in

Your journal entries listing goals related to your passions will be unique and reflect your hopes for the future. You may also want to periodically update and elaborate on your goals and objectives as you learn more about yourself and the best way to achieve goals related to your passions. With careful planning, you can find ways to ensure that the things you are passionate about become an important part of your life.

Communicating Passion

While it is important for leaders to understand their passions, they must also be able to communicate their passions to others. It is not enough for leaders to feel passionate about something. They must also inform others that they believe something is worth caring about. As a result, communication skills are essential for understanding how to lead with passion.

To be an effective leader, you must make a decision to communicate your passions to others. If you are indeed passionate about a subject, you will be naturally animated and enthusiastic when discussing the subject. There are also times when you may have to be more restrained when discussing a topic — based on the situation. Part of the skills necessary to communicate your passion to others is the ability to determine how much information you should convey and how enthusiastic you should be in different situations.

An approach to communicating passion is to create a vision for the future and to inform others about the importance and benefits of putting your vision into action. This approach requires that you have a clear understanding of the short-term and long-term goals related to your passion. It also requires that you carefully select the amount of information you provide to others about the goals to ensure that they perceive the way they will benefit from achieving the goal. You should also be aware that others often find it easier to understand small, short-term goals that are easy to obtain rather than large goals that are more difficult to achieve. The amount of passion you use when communicating your vision for the future is important for building trust among potential followers.

Using Passion to Build Trust

Passion nurtures a desire to share your values with others, which is important for building trust. Values are the beliefs of a particular society or cultural group. These beliefs determine the types of behaviors that are considered desirable or undesirable. For example, honesty is usually a desirable value, while dishonesty is an undesirable value.

Individuals are more likely to trust someone who has the same values. When discussing your passions with others, your values become clear. Your passion for a topic can show values — such as compassion or respect for tradition — that others may respect and share. When others become aware of your values, they believe that you will act in accordance with the values. Your behaviors are more predictable, and your motivations are more transparent. As a result, communicating your values helps to build trust, because followers assume that the goals the leader pursues are in line with the leader's values.

Your passion for something also communicates how real you are. It is difficult to fake passion, because it is an emotion that is often natural. From this perspective, the passion you demonstrate leads others to be certain that you genuinely believe in the beneficial nature of the goal you are trying to achieve. They are more likely to trust that you will remain dedicated to achieving the goal. If others trust you, you can more easily influence others.

Using Passion to Inspire Others

"Just don't give up trying to do what you really want to do. Where there is love and inspiration, I don't think you can go wrong."

— *ELLA FITZGERALD*

Not all followers will share your passion, regardless of the degree of trust they feel for your skills as a communicator. For example, your passion may lead to emotional commitment to an organization. Other members of the organization may share your values and trust you but not feel the same level of commitment to the organization. An effective leader must be able to recognize the passions of others — even when these passions are different and related to dissimilar values. You may be faced with a situation in which you have to ignite the passion of followers to achieve your goal by explaining to them how the goal will coincide with their passions. This approach can be considered proactive leadership, because you are attempting to leverage the passions of others to establish and achieve a common goal.

Your passion can ignite a vision for the future you can share with others. The vision often involves a change from the current situation to a more desirable future situation. Using your passion to inspire others requires some degree of natural enthusiasm to allow others to take action. If your passion becomes infectious and inspires others, they will want to participate in the effort to achieve the shared vision. As a result, you can use your passion to prompt others to act.

Passion can take many forms, such as providing encouragement, teaching others what must be done, and allowing others to make decisions without you guiding them. In practice, this approach may include fostering the leadership development of other individuals who share your passion. When others are inspired to pursue a vision for the future, they become self-motivated and want to act on their own initiative.

Summary

Passionate leadership requires both an understanding of your own passion and an understanding of the passions of others. If you know what ignites your interests and passions, you can more easily communicate your passion to others. Passion can help build trust between leaders and followers, because it involves a genuine expression of the way people feel about something. It is also evidence of an individual's commitment. Leaders can use their passion to inspire others to adopt a shared vision and to strive toward achieving the vision. A leader should also make an effort to understand the passions of followers and give them tasks that suit their interests.

"I did *30-Minute Meals* for five years on local television, and I earned nothing the first two years. Then, I earned $50 a segment. I spent more than that on gas and groceries, but I really enjoyed making the show, and I loved going to a viewer's house each week. I knew I enjoyed it, so I stuck with it even though it cost me."

— Rachael Ray

Case Study 3: Communicating Passion in a University

Michael has just been appointed as chair of the Faculty of Education at a prestigious independent university. The department consists of many professors who have been with the university for many years and an equal number of adjunct professors who are relatively new employees. He has been employed as a professor at the university for about five years and has a reputation for pursuing excellence in education. He has also been responsible for many initiatives in the School of Education, such as the introduction of online instruction for some courses.

Michael was not a popular choice to chair the department among the more seasoned faculty members. They believed that he was not sufficiently committed to the traditions and reputation of the university. They also believed that he had the long-term goal of altering the philosophy of the Department of Education, which they perceived as a potential difficulty, because it would require changing their traditional methods of education. This group valued conformity and security. Some of the senior faculty were also displeased that they had not been selected for the position. They believed that Michael's efforts to stimulate change in the department were deceitful and intended only to ensure he received the appointment as chair of the department.

In contrast, Michael was a popular choice among the adjunct faculty to chair the department. These younger professors shared many of his ideas concerning the future of education and wanted to be certain that their students were prepared to meet new challenges. They also believed that Michael cared about the students and wanted to modernize the teaching methods. Many of these younger professors were successful in using the techniques that Michael advocated, such as online instruction. This group placed greater emphasis on autonomy and self-direction in the university environment.

Michael was uncertain about how to proceed. He believed that enrollment in the Department of Education would suffer if the teaching content and methods did not keep up with the times. Although he chaired the department, he could not make major changes without the support of most of the senior faculty. He also wanted to end the growing factionalism between the seasoned professors and the adjunct faculty.

Questions:

1. Is Michael passionate about the university? Provide evidence explaining why he is or is not passionate about the university.
2. How can Michael communicate any passion he feels about the university or the Department of Education to the senior faculty?
3. How can Michael build trust with the senior members of the faculty?
4. What steps can Michael take to leverage any passion he feels about the university or the Department of Education to influence all members of the faculty?

Chapter 4: Critical Thinking

"Too often we…enjoy the comfort of opinion without the
discomfort of thought."
—John F. Kennedy

Do you know many young people fail to think? Do you
know that in some cultures being a critical thinker is
considered disrespectful? However, in universities critical
thinking is an important skill to develop. Critical thinking is
about asking questions and then making evaluations. The
process of critical thinking is important to use while attending
university and in your everyday life. Often when students
first enroll at university they are more familiar with
summarizing or reciting information and ideas. Critical
thinking is a skill which is difficult for all students. This is
because students are required to develop their own results or
views.

Characteristics of Critical Thinking
To become a critical thinker, you must develop a few skills.
Recognize assumptions you carry with you.
Have you ever wondered why you believe the things that you
believe? Do you believe things because you've been told to
believe them? You need to step outside your own
philosophies or point of view to observe from a neutral
standpoint. Try not to make assumption.

You need to process information justly.
People sometimes pass along information that is false. People
spread rumors on Facebook, Twitter, Instagram, etc. We're
guilty of reading posts that are incorrect and passing them
along without checking for the truth.

Recognize a generalization.
Girls don't like watching sports. Old people are educated.
Cats make better pets. These statements are generalizations
and are not always true.
Produce new ideas based on sound evidence.
Detectives solve crimes by collecting evidence. The entire
truth-seeking process is weakened by one piece of bad
evidence, and this leads to a wrong conclusion.
Analyze a problem and recognize the complex parts.
Judge your sources.
Learn to recognize hidden agendas and biases when you
collect information.
As students progress from high school into college and
graduate school they must develop critical thinking skills in
order to carry out research. Students will learn to identify
good sources and bad sources, and make logical conclusions
and develop new theories.
 Here is an example of critical thinking in practice:
One day Socrates, the great philosopher, came upon an
acquaintance that ran up to him eagerly and said, "Socrates,
do you know what I just heard about one of your students?"
"Wait a moment," Socrates replied. "Before you tell me I'd like
you to pass a little test. It's called the Triple Filter Test."
"Triple filter?"

"That's right," Socrates continued. "Before you talk to me
about my student let's take a moment to filter what you're
going to say. The first filter is Truth. Have you made
absolutely sure that what you are about to tell me is true?"
"No," the man said, "actually I just heard about it and..."
"All right," said Socrates. "So you don't really know if it's true
or not. Now let's try the second filter, the filter of Goodness. Is
what you are about to tell me about my student something
good?"
"No, on the contrary..."

"So," Socrates continued, "you want to tell me something bad about him, even though you're not certain it's true?" The man shrugged, a little embarrassed. Socrates continued. "You may still pass the test though, because there is a third filter - the filter of Usefulness. Is what you want to tell me about my student going to be useful to me?"

"No, not really"

"Well," concluded Socrates, "if what you want to tell me is neither true nor good nor even useful, why tell it to me at all?" The man walked away deflated.

In this story Socrates lays out a set of criteria for determining whether or not it's right to tell someone something about someone else. In this case the criteria are: is it true, is it good, and is it useful.

Learning how to think critically can improve your decision-making processes and help you become a better leader. Leaders are inherently responsible for making decisions—with the decisions often related to solving a problem that stops the followers from achieving a goal. The critical-thinking process primarily provides a structure based on reason for solving problems. As a result, the leader can justify the belief or action that is the product of critical thinking, because other reasonable people in the same situation could come to the same conclusion. It also strengthens your ability to collect and evaluate information, which is a necessary process when making even minor decisions.

Critical thinking can also foster creativity, because it attempts to identify and analyze many possible solutions to a problem. As a result, it increases the potential for identifying a new approach that has not been tried in the past to solve a problem. Whenever faced with a problem, you should consider it an opportunity to use critical thinking to show your leadership ability through the quality of your judgments. Using a wise approach to solving the problem by collecting and analyzing information indicates that you have the competencies expected of a leader. In addition, the critical-thinking process uses many of the same skills that are linked with leadership, such as communication, relationship building, and problem solving. A critical-thinking approach is also likely to result in a better understanding of the situation in which you are expected to lead, which will improve the overall quality of your leadership.

Developing Critical-Thinking Skills

Everyone can improve his/her critical-thinking skills with practice. Critical-thinking skills involve thoughtful analysis of information rather than an emotional response. You should think with clear well-defined points that are connected. As with other leadership skills, critical-thinking skills can be learned by relying on an established system for identifying and analyzing information. By understanding the nature of critical-thinking skills, you can gradually increase your ability to use a structured process when faced with the need to reach a decision.

When faced with a complex problem, you can use several techniques to identify the root cause of the problem. The most basic technique is to gather information to ensure that the problem exists. If there is a genuine problem, the way you define the problem can affect the type of questions that you ask to solve the problem. As a result, you should not define the problem based on preconceived ideas about the nature of the problem and possible solutions. With complex problems, it may also be beneficial to divide the larger problem into sub-problems. It can sometimes be difficult to understand the root cause of a problem if it involves many activities or functions that are related parts of a large system. It may also be helpful for you to make a model or diagram of the problem to help see in your mind the possible causes.

Critical Thinking Exercise

FACT AND OPINION
A fact is something that is true or can be proven. An opinion is your feelings or how someone else feels about a specific topic. *Read the sentences below and indicate whether each is a fact or an opinion by writing fact or opinion on the lines provided.*

Abraham Lincoln was President of the United States during the Civil War. _____
My favorite singer is Beyoncé. _____
Thanksgiving is celebrated in November in America.
_____
Students must pass a graduation test in Florida. _____
My mother is the best cook. _____
Students achieving A Honor Roll for the first semester will be recognized for their hard work. _____
My dad feels all students should be required to wear school uniforms. _____
George Washington Carver was a famous inventor.
_____

All boys like football game. _____
The Presidential Election is held in November. _____

Summary

Critical thinking involves using a reflective and logical strategy to collect and assess information necessary to make decisions or come to your own conclusion. Critical thinking improves leadership abilities, because leaders are required to analyze information and make reasonable decisions. Critical thinking requires stopping judgment during the time you collect your evidence. Critical-thinking skills can be learned and generally involve a framework involving the cause of a problem, collecting information, analyzing information, and drawing conclusions from the analysis.

Case Study 4: Analyzing a Sales Problem

Lakeisha has been recently hired as the sales and marketing director for a medium-sized manufacturing firm that produces piping for commercial customers. Although she has prior experience in commercial marketing, she is not familiar with the operations of the firm or its customer base. She is responsible for supervising a staff of seven employees; five of them are engaged in outside sales.

Shortly after beginning her first day of work, Lakeisha is called into the office of the firm's CEO, who describes a particular problem with the sales and marketing department. According to the CEO:

For the last few months, we have been getting too many special orders from our customers. We've always had a policy of accommodating special orders — especially if the customer is willing to pay more but the setup time for these special orders is getting in the way of our regular production schedule. I don't know why we're getting so many special orders. Maybe it's because your sales people get a higher commission on the special orders. Maybe it's because there's some change in the customer needs that we don't know about. What I want you to do is find out why this is happening and figure out a solution. We don't want to alienate our customers. At the same time, we can't afford to keep changing our production line setup.

Questions:
1. How should Lakeisha go about gathering information necessary to identify the root cause of the problem?
2. With whom should Lakeisha consult concerning the possible solutions to the problem?
3. How should Lakeisha justify to the CEO any decision concerning solutions to the problem?

Chapter 5: How to Be a Better Decision Maker

"Where there is no decision there is no life."
—J. J. Dewey

Making decisions is a key part of leadership. Even when a leader uses a laissez-faire leadership style, the leader remains responsible for making many decisions, such as the nature of the goals that followers should pursue and the type of leadership style that is appropriate for the situation. Followers often look to leaders to make decisions — particularly if they have difficulty with imagining the specific tasks that are needed to achieve a goal. Because of the importance of decision making to leadership, you should understand how to approach decision making.

To make better decisions, you should understand that decision making is a process involving a sequential series of steps that are often considered part of the critical-thinking process. These steps are 1) identify the problem, 2) analyze the possible solutions to the problem, 3) evaluate which of the possible solutions will be most effective, and 4) select and implement the solution. These steps give you a structured framework to improve the quality of your decisions. The first three steps focus on collecting information that is useful when making a decision. The way leaders, as decision makers, collect the information often depends on their leadership style and the situation. For example, the autocratic leader may be comfortable with personally collecting the information, while a participative leader may be comfortable relying on the information provided by others.

Identifying a problem requires that you understand that a problem exists and can recognize the root cause of the problem. While it is often easy to recognize the symptoms of a problem, the actual cause of the problem may not be clear. As a result, a good leader carefully evaluates the nature of the problem before considering the possible solutions.

All problems have more than one possible solution. Effective decision making requires recognizing the possible solutions that address the cause of the problem. The analysis determines the way each of the possible solutions will affect the problem. The analysis should also include the effect of the possible solution on the processes or systems used by an organization based on the assumption that a change to fix one part of a system may cause a new problem with another part of the system. After evaluating the possible options, the leader should be able to determine the solution that is most likely to solve the problem without causing new and unexpected problems.

A leader responsible for making decisions should also recognize that all decisions will not produce the desired result. Some solutions appear effective in theory but fail in practice. As a result, an effective decision maker has a contingency plan in the event that the decision fails to achieve the desired result. The likely plan often consists of a solution to the problem that was rejected during the evaluation phase of the decision-making process.

Decision-Making Process
Step 1. Identify the problem
Step 2. Brainstorm for possible solutions
Step 3. Evaluate the positive and negative consequences of each solution
Step 4. Select the solution
Step 5. Take responsibility for the decision

Case Study 5: Decisions, Decisions

Roy loves bikes. He wishes he could have all the bikes he wants. Unfortunately, he can't; he has two brothers and three sisters, and his parents cannot afford to buy all their children designer bikes. Roy has a few friends who have bikes. His friends let him borrow their bikes, even though this is against his parents' wishes. His parents feel that Roy should not borrow them in case something was to happen to them. In that case, they would need to purchase a new bike to replace the damaged one. One day on the way home from school, Roy tripped and fell on his knees. He had twisted the wheels of the bike he had borrowed from his friend, Matt. Roy was in pain, not only because he had injured his knees, but because the bike was ruined.

Questions:
1. Should Roy tell his parents?

2. Should he tell Matt?

3. What decisions should Roy have made prior to

   borrowing the bike?

4. Does Roy have an obligation to Matt?

Chapter 6: Group Work, Team Work, Make the Dream Work

"Talent wins games, but teamwork and intelligence wins championships."

—Michael Jordan

A group or team is combined of a number of individuals who share a common goal. A team can produce more through a joint effort than the individual members of the team could produce by working alone. The effectiveness of the group or team can be determined by its level of success in achieving the common goal. Many things can influence the effectiveness of the group or team, such as the knowledge and skills of individual team members and the level of trust and support among the members. Understanding the function of the leader in assisting the group or team to achieve its goals is an important leadership skill.

Bella loves fashion. She attended a school for fashion design. Eager to get her fashion designs exposed to the public, Bella decided to invest in trade shows to exhibit and sell some of the products she had created. However, as a recent graduate, she didn't have the money required to be successful at the trade shows, and her parents could raise only $5,000 of the $20,000 Bella needed. Additionally, she was unable to secure a loan because she did not have a job. Bella thought that if she didn't participate in these trade shows she might never get the chance to exhibit her designs and make money.

Bella called her friend Rochelle to see if she would partner with her at the trade shows. Rochelle was excited about the idea, but she had only a $5,000 gift she'd recently received from her grandfather. Rochelle designs accessories and was nervous to invest more than $5,000. Both Bella and Rochelle decided that if they were going to do these trade shows, they would need two other like-minded individuals with different products to complement what they would sell. Bella and Rochelle called on Mark, a shoe designer, and Annie, a bag designer, to be a part of their group. Although the terms *group* and *team* are often used interchangeably, the two concepts are distinct. A group consists of individuals working independently in an organization. Although the members of the group work toward achieving a common goal, each individual is relatively indifferent to the tasks performed by other members of the group. A team consists of individuals working in concert to achieve a common goal. The work performed by each team member is interdependent with the work performed by other members. The combined efforts of the team determine if it is successful in achieving its objectives. Because of the differences between a group and a team, leaders have to use different approaches to motivate and inspire followers.

Group Leadership

A group usually has a strong and designated leader. As such, Bella took the leader role since this was initially her idea and she had to make sure everything ran smoothly. The effectiveness of the group in achieving objectives depends on the ability of the leader to coordinate the activities of its members. To accomplish this, the leader of a group forms individual relationships with each of the group members.

The leader has to determine the best method to motivate individual followers to perform the tasks necessary to reach the common objective based on the characteristics of the follower and the demands of the situation.

If the group is large, the leader cannot easily establish and maintain relationships with each group member and may have to delegate leadership responsibilities to others. The leader of the group is responsible for ensuring that the members are accountable for the tasks they perform. At the same time, the leader establishes the performance goals for the members of the group and monitors whether they comply with the goals. In this context, the leader has to ensure that the performance goals are realistic and can be achieved by the members of the group. At the same time, the leader has to motivate the members of the group to achieve their individual performance goals.

Team Leadership

Team leadership is more complex than group leadership, because the leader has to influence the team as a whole — as well as each member of the team. Team leadership can be defined in terms of the functions of the leader. The leader has a task function of ensuring that the team members are motivated to perform the tasks necessary to achieve the objective. The leader also has a relationship function, which consists of ensuring that the team members have the ability and skills to work together as a team. In the team, the leader forms dyadic relationships with team members and a separate relationship with the team as a whole.

Team Development

Effective teams do not occur naturally. A team must be built by leaders who take the actions necessary to bring the team members together and support their ability to work together to reach a common goal. In some situations, the leader must create a team from a group, with the members of the team retaining the individualistic performance perspective characteristic of the group. The stage of development of the team often affects the actions the leader must take to support smooth functioning of the team. One model of team development suggests that there are four stages: forming, storming, norming, and performing.

Forming

In the initial stage of team development, form or create the team members. The team must meet and exchange information about behaviors they consider acceptable. The leader's role in this stage of team development is to facilitate communication to assist the team with establishing explicit and implicit guidelines for behavior and methods for performing tasks.

Storming

This stage often involves discussions and disagreements about the nature of the task and how to perform the task. Team members may form subgroups based on their respective positions concerning roles and approaches to the task. The leader's role during this stage is particularly critical, because some teams do not progress out of this stage if they do not reach an agreement on how to achieve the team objective.

Norming

The next stage of team development, norming, involves the cooperation of the members. The team members organize themselves to complete the tasks necessary to meet the objectives of the team. The team members also demonstrate increased concern for other team members to ensure that they are performing their tasks. As a result, this stage involves increased identification of the individual members with the team. This fosters the ability of the team to use social pressure to encourage conformity with team behavioral norms. The role of the leader in this stage of team development is to ensure that the norms established by the team will support the ability of the team to achieve its objective.

Performing

The final stage of team development is performing, in which the team is functioning effectively and progressing toward achieving its goal. The team members are working together with great flexibility and cohesion, and the team members are focused on both the task and the relationships among team members. Because the team is self-motivated and self-directed at this stage, leadership becomes less important. The leader's role becomes more facilitative; for example, the leader ensures that the team members remain balanced between the task and relationship activities.

In addition to the changes in the leader's role due to changes in the stages of team development, the leader's role can also evolve based on the type of function or purpose of the team. A functional team is formed to perform a task in a specific functional area — with the members of the team often having similar functional skills.

An example of this type of team is a production team in which all the members have similar skills related to the production activity. The functional team is generally leader-centered, although the members of the team are accustomed to acting collaboratively in the same functional area. This type of team often needs traditional leadership in which the leader forms strong relationships with each member of the team as well as a relationship with the group as a whole.

Team-Building Activities

Team-building activities are intended to remind the members of a team about the importance of working together to achieve a common objective. These activities are useful for leaders in the forming and norming stages of team development, because they increase the degree of trust among the team members and in the abilities of the team leader. They also stimulate social interactions among the team members, which are helpful for the informal relationships necessary for effective teamwork. There are many different team-building activities that build team cohesion. The following activities are intended to give you an idea of the various approaches a leader can select to help develop a team.

Getting Acquainted

Purpose: This activity is useful in the early forming stage of team development to help the members become familiar with the other team members.

Materials: None

Activity: Have each person identify himself or herself in terms of an inanimate object such as a chair or table. This inanimate object should symbolize or describe some aspect of his or her personality or identity. Each person should also be able to explain the reason he or she selected the inanimate object. This approach creates a unique method for the members of the team to understand each other in a way that may not be obvious to outsiders. It also may demonstrate some of the strengths and weaknesses of the individuals in the team as well as their ability to think creatively.

Building Trust: Minefields

Purpose: This activity is helpful in the norming stage of team development for enabling the team members to understand the way they must rely on each other to achieve a common goal.

Materials: Small brightly colored objects such as toy blocks and blindfolds

Activity: The team members are randomly placed into subteams. One member of the subteam is blindfolded. The team leader then scatters the brightly colored objects around an indoor or outdoor area. The individual without the blindfold must verbally provide directions to the person with the blindfold to guide him or her through the minefield. The activity demonstrates the coordination necessary among team members.

Building Trust and Coordination: Paper Towers

Purpose: This activity helps the members of a team work together to perform a task. It should be used with large teams that can be grouped into subteams of three people.

Materials: One sheet of sturdy paper for each member of the team

Activity: Each team must build a tower made of paper in five minutes using no other materials. The team constructing the highest tower is deemed the winner. Afterward, all team members should discuss issues, such as the strategy they used, the reasons for success or failure, and the way they would approach the task in the future. The team should also examine how they worked together under a time constraint.

Conflict and Leadership

Group dynamics involve the relationships among the members of a group or team as well as the relationships of the members with the leader. The relationships create a dynamic that the leader must manage to maximize the effectiveness of the group or team. Because human relationships are complex, various types of situations or problems can arise to produce conflict that the leader must understand and react to by influencing individual members of the group or team.

Conflict is normal in a group or team. For example, there can be disagreements about the approach to solve a problem or perform a task among members; this is a natural outcome when a complex issue arises. Conversely, the absence of conflict can be an indication that the team is not functioning properly, because agreement may be the result of an authoritarian leader or of another factor. The appropriate role for the leader of the group or team is to assist the members to work through the conflict to achieve consensus that supports cooperation.

The conflict dynamic in a group generally involves differences between the individual members of the team and the team leader. When managing conflict in a group, the leader can use various approaches that are suited to the specific characteristics of the follower such as becoming more directive or allowing the follower to participate in the decision-making process. In a team, the conflict occurs among the members of the team with different causes, depending on the stage of development. In the storming stage, for example, conflicts stem from disagreements about the roles of the members of the group and the implicit rules governing relationships. In the performing stage of development, conflict arises from disagreements concerning the way tasks should be performed.

The role of the leader is to manage — rather than eliminate — conflicts. Conflicts become unhealthy for the group or team only if they are so severe as to undermine cooperative working relationships. At the same time, a normal amount of conflict is beneficial, because it can contribute to innovation. A particularly important function of the leader for managing conflict in a team is assisting the members to identify the source of the conflict. The source of conflict may not be obvious. The leader should ensure that the members of a team avoid personal attacks when expressing disagreements.

Activities to Help Resolve Conflict

Developing the skills to resolve conflicts can be difficult if you have not had experience with team leadership and managing the different personalities that are part of a team. There are several activities that you can use, however, that can help you manage conflicts in your daily life. These conflicts need not be major but can, nonetheless, be helpful, because conflict resolution processes are similar — regardless of the magnitude of the conflict.

Journaling

For a week, keep a journal of any issues you experience involving conflict with others. The journal should record your perception of the situation, your emotional response, and your understanding of the cause of the conflict. At the end of the week, you can reflect on methods you could use to resolve the conflict, such as changing your behaviors or discussing the issue with the other party to the conflict. If you are a leader of a team, you can also ask the members of the team to use a journal to record the events surrounding conflicts. By using the information in the journal as a basis for discussions with team members, you can help to resolve the conflict.

Role Reversal

Role reversal involves posing a scenario to team members who may be in conflict over an issue. One person assumes a role in the scenario and acts out the role. For example, this person may be given the role of a managing team member who has just identified a major error by another team member. Afterward, the other person attempts to mimic the way the first person acted. This type of activity is intended to provide members of the team with insights about the way other team members view them. It helps to change some of the behaviors contributing to conflicts.

Mediation

This activity requires at least three people, with one person acting as mediator while the other two act as team members with a dispute, for example, a disagreement about work habits such as timely completion of tasks. The role of the mediator is not to decide the issue in dispute, but rather to assist the individuals in conflict to develop a resolution that is mutually agreeable to each party. The mediator ensures that each party to the dispute presents his or her arguments and appreciates the perspective of the other party. The role of mediator is fundamentally a team leadership task to assist team members to work together in achieving the common team goal.

Power and Social Influence

Power is the ability to change the behaviors, beliefs, or attitudes of others based on an individual's personal authority or the authority inherent in the position the individual occupies in an organization. Social influence is the ability to change the behaviors, beliefs, or attitudes of others based on the pressure to conform created by a group. A formal leader can exert influence over the group or team based on the power inherent in the position of team leader. In a team, the members use influence over each other based on their ability to use social influence. In a group, the ability to use social influence is minimal, because the group members do not have close relationships with each other.

Bella, Rochelle, Mark, and Annie experienced some issues at the trade shows but quickly resolved them. Bella took the leadership roll so that things could run effectively. They focused on their mission and were able to make a profit. The group continued to work together in trade shows for years. Bella and Rochelle opened a small boutique that has done well.

Summary

Members of a group work independently and have a direct relationship with the group leader. Leading teams is more complex than leading groups because of the dynamics that can develop among the members. Teams go through stages of development with the role of the leader changing in each stage.

Case Study 6: Team Decisions at Lukoil

Ali has just been appointed project director to coordinate the activities of a fifteen-person exploration team at Lukoil. The project mission is to make initial assessments of various sites that may be suitable for oil extraction. The team has been together for more than a year but has had three previous project managers during this time. The reports indicate that the team has been performing effectively and has identified one site that could potentially be developed for oil production. The team members will receive a bonus if they find a suitable location for future development. Ali has various degrees in geology and some previous experience on exploration teams in other firms. He is, however, much younger than the members of the Lukoil team.

After meeting with the team, he suspects that most of the decisions are made by an older geologist whom the other team members respect. He also discovers that there is a dispute among some members of the team concerning whether to abandon their current region for exploration activities or to continue in the same area for several more months. The older geologist suggests moving to another area—most of the team agrees. A minority of the team, however, is adamant in the belief that continued exploration in the current area will eventually find oil.

After reviewing all the available data, Ali agrees with the minority of team members who believe that the assessment of the area should continue. As a new team leader, he has the authority to order the team to continue exploration in the current area. He is concerned, however, that this approach would alienate the older geologist and his ability to influence the team members who support his position.

Questions:
1. What is the stage of team development? What is the role of the leader in this stage of development?

2. What are the possible approaches Ali can use to resolve the conflict between the two factions? Which approach should he use?
3. What are the sources of Ali's power in the team? How can he effectively use these sources of power to lead the team in the current situation?

Chapter 7: Present Values People Will Believe In

"We can tell our values by looking at our checkbook stubs."
— Gloria Steinem

It is important for young leaders to embrace a set of values that others consider important and desirable. Values are beliefs and judgments that provide guidelines for behaviors. In the context of leadership, values tend to function as an ethical measure. Followers tend to recognize leaders who show higher level of values as being trustworthy. Followers will also admire individuals who live by the socially desirable values and will consider them very good leaders. In contrast, followers are less likely to accept the leadership of individuals who fail to show socially desirable values. For example, followers generally expect leaders to display integrity and loyalty. These are essential for followers to accept the realness of the leader. Leaders develop values from their beliefs and convictions — with values and passion often intertwined. As a result, leaders must understand their personal values and how they contribute to effective leadership.

For you to lead, it is not enough to have values. You must also communicate these values to others so that they are reasonably assured that you are acting for the greater good. You should not only state your values but live by them as well. Your actions must indicate to followers that you 'live what you preach'- your values. When there is a situation involving a conflict among values, followers must also understand the way you prioritize values to ensure a fair and equitable outcome.

In leadership, values drive commitment. The way you present values to others can determine their level of trust in your leadership abilities. People are more willing to follow leaders who demonstrate the same values, because their actions are more predictable. A leader who is perceived as trustworthy because of his or her values can more easily influence others because of the assumption that the leader is acting in a principled manner.

Communicating Values People Believe In

There are many different values recognized by different societies; some have estimated that there are well over one hundred different values. Yet only a few values are very important to most leaders. These are the core values that provide a foundation for principled action. Because of the many different values that people can embrace, it is unlikely that followers will have exactly the same set of important values as you — even if they come from the same culture and social group.

A leader does not attempt to impose values on followers, because any attempt to change values is likely to result in bitterness. Values — and the way an individual prioritizes values — are very personal. Many people consider their values important to their character. Attempts to influence others to change their values and value priority can reduce trust in a leader and commitment to the leader's goals and objectives.

The differences in values among individuals, however, do not create an impossible barrier to leadership. People recognize that others may have different values and often establish different priorities among the values. They are willing to accept these differences as long as they do not result in a significant conflict with their own values. At the same time, a leader must communicate values to others to allow them to evaluate the values and determine if they are similar to or different from their own values. From this perspective, one of the fundamental tasks of leadership is gaining consensus concerning the way the group values are related to the common cause.

An approach to communicating values that others can believe in is to consider communication as a three-step process. In the first step, you have to be clear about your personal values and make them known to others. In the second step, you have to listen to others to learn about their values and the value priorities. Because most people have not considered their values, this second step may involve careful observation of others over a period of time. This step is particularly important because of the need for leaders to ensure that they do not ask followers to act in a manner that conflicts with their values. In the third step, you have to ensure that the vision for the future that you express to others conforms to both your own values and the values of your followers. In effect, others must recognize that the objective you propose that others work toward does not conflict with their values.

When you communicate values to others verbally, a simple approach is best. The language should be plain and direct such as, "I believe integrity is an important value." Attempting to use slang or a complex approach to expressing your values to others is likely to be confusing.

Values are highly abstract concepts that have different shades of meaning based on the culture and experiences of individuals. As a result, merely stating that you value honesty does not effectively describe what you mean when you are expressing the value. Honesty can mean avoiding deceit, avoiding theft, speaking plainly and frankly, or acting fairly.

Identifying Your Leadership Values

As a leader, you may have many different values that affect your focus on leadership tasks and your relationships with others. These values are convictions about the things you believe are important and desirable in your behaviors and your approach to leadership. At the same time, you should clarify the values that are vital for you so you develop better self-understanding and credibility as a leader by applying these values to leadership situations. Understanding your values can also help you prioritize tasks and resolve ethical issues when you act in leadership roles.

Activity: Understanding Your Values

Purpose: To clarify the basic values motivating you

Activity: Below is a list of values associated with leadership. You should select five of the values that best complete the following sentence: _____ is important to my approach to leadership. After selecting five values, write a few sentences discussing why you believe the value is important to your approach to leadership.
(If this activity is undertaken by groups, it would also be helpful to have the group members discuss why a particular value is important to an understanding of leadership.)

Integrity   Friendliness
                             Predictability
Responsibility   Trust
                             Wisdom
Adventure   Reassurance
                             Responsiveness
Loyalty   Order
                             Honesty
Industriousness   Security
                             Independence
Self-Respect   Freedom
                             Fairness
Balance   Expertise
                             Creativity
Cooperation   Control
                             Challenge
Conformity   Personal Development
                             Accountability
Ethics   Flexibility
                             Courage
Humility   Persistence
                             Consistency
Tradition   Benevolence
                             Enthusiasm
Happiness   Diversity
                             Helpfulness

Representing Values by Example

The most effective means of representing values that others will believe in is by example. The example set by leaders overrides other forms of communication and becomes the main way that followers assess the values of the leader. In practical situations, representing values by living the values not only communicates your core values to others but can also be a source of influence, because followers may want to emulate your example. In the long run, the actions of the leader will demonstrate his or her values and degree of commitment to them.

In general, a leader who behaves in a manner contrary to espoused values and the vision the leader has encouraged others to adopt will send a strong negative message to followers. A leader claiming to espouse a value accepted by others while acting contrary to the value will lose credibility. For example, a leader cannot claim to prioritize the value of honesty if the leader engages in deceitful behaviors.

It is important for leaders to be aware of the relationship between their values and their actions to ensure that inconsistencies do not arise. In some situations, an inconsistency between value and behavior can occur if there is a conflict in the priority of values. Let's return to the example of the leader who, based on the value of duty, terminates a poorly performing employee in order to protect the group — despite the leader's espoused value of loyalty. Some followers may view this action inconsistent with the leader's stated values. In this situation, the leader has to directly address the apparent inconsistency in behavior by explaining the nature of the conflict in values and the priority of values that guided the decision. If the leader fails to address the apparent inconsistency, followers may believe that the leader is not sincere in the claim of principled leadership based on values.

When the follower admires the leader, there is greater willingness to emulate the behavior of the leader, including the apparent commitment of the leader to specific values. This influence over the values of followers occurs when the leader's values are similar to the values of the followers. In addition, followers are more likely to adopt the values of the leader when they perceive the leader as charismatic. A charismatic leader exhibits great enthusiasm for achieving a vision of the future, places a large amount of trust in subordinates, and leads by example (Bass and Bass 2008).

Leadership Principles and Your Behavior

A good leader has the ability to translate leadership principles or values into behaviors that others recognize and consider as attributes of a good leader. The leader's behaviors provide an example to others and build trust in the leader's abilities. A leader must understand his or her core principles or values and the way these principles affect his or her behaviors. The following activity will help you identify your values and understand their relationship to leadership behaviors.

Putting Your Values into Practice

Purpose: The purpose of this activity is to help you determine ways you use leadership practices that incorporate your values. It can also help you understand the variety of ways you can use leadership values in practice.

Activity: On the left side of the chart below are several values. There are also several blank areas on the left side for other values you may believe are important for good leadership. Complete the chart by thinking of at least one way you can put the value into practice as a leader.

(If this activity is performed by a group, it is helpful to discuss the way that individuals can put the different leadership values into practice with specific behaviors.)

Leadership Values	Leadership Behaviors Related to the Value
Responsiveness	
Authenticity	
Integrity	
Accountability	
Excellence	
Positive Intentions	

Summary

Leaders are more likely to influence followers when they adhere to a set of values that are similar to the values of the followers and that result in predictable behaviors. Effective leaders must understand their own values as well as the values of followers. In addition, effective leaders must ensure that the vision they present does not conflict with the values of the followers. To turn values into action, leaders should develop principles, which are guidelines to ensure that behaviors are consistent with values. Principles also assist with prioritizing values when a conflict among values arises. Communicating values should be based on a three-step process of understanding your turn values, understanding your followers' values, and ensuring that a vision communicated to others conforms to their values. Representing values by example is the most effective approach in communicating values—with actions demonstrating the leader's commitment to values.

Case Study 7: A Clash of Values

Kevin is the head of the planning division of a large municipal government, supervising a staff of twenty-five employees. He is very reserved and formal, acting in a distant but professional manner with his staff. At the same time, he is deeply committed to values such as integrity, community service, and loyalty, which he believes are values absolutely necessary for effectiveness in all government operations. He is also attempting to improve the quality of the output in the planning division, with quality determined by the accuracy of the forecasts produced by the division.

Although Kevin has been head of the planning division for more than a year, the employees believe that he is excessively formal and that he does not listen to their needs. His behaviors often seem unpredictable. On one occasion, he reprimanded a group of employees because they left work early to attend a party for one of the workers. He indicated that taking pay for time when they were not at work was similar to theft from the employer. At other times, however, he has allowed workers to leave the office during working hours to tend to personal family matters.

Kevin's actions have affected the employees' perception of him to the point that he is unable to motivate the workers in the planning division. At meetings, they are reluctant to interact with him and behave as if they do not trust his judgment. The workers in the planning division are reluctant to communicate problems and resource needs to Kevin. Some of the workers believe that his efforts to improve quality in the planning division are intended only to improve his chances for promotion and advancement and not to benefit other divisions that rely on planning services.

Kevin recognized that the employees were not committed to his quality initiatives for the planning division and that they often avoided interacting with him. He also believed that many employees did not share his values — which required him to closely supervise the employees. Despite these issues, he wondered if his approach to leadership was contributing to the low level of commitment and negative behaviors of the employees.

Questions:

1. How can Kevin determine if his values are aligned with the values of the employees in the planning division?
2. What steps can Kevin take to improve the way he communicates his values to his employees?
3. How can Kevin communicate his principles and the way he resolves conflicts between values?

Chapter 8: Working in the Community

"Teaching kids how to feed themselves and how to live in a community responsibly is the center of an education."

—Alice Waters

David's love is his neighborhood in Queens, New York. He was born in that neighborhood and lived there with his parents before attending a college in Florida to study law. During his time in college, his focus was on his studies and he did not realize that his beloved neighborhood had taken a turn for the worse. He graduated cum laude and was praised by many who knew him. At twenty-three years of age David passed the bar exam and got a good job in Manhattan, New York. His parents were excited as their son was making a name for himself as a successful attorney.

Although David had a good job, he decided to stay at home with his parents. He then started to realize that his neighborhood was not as safe as it was before he left college. David decided to go to community watch meetings where he realized how being involved would be important to his development. David's passion for his community was so deep that he went out of his way to protect the good citizens in his neighborhood. Working in the community is very important to your professional development. Whether you volunteer at a senior citizen home or assist with a campaign for breast cancer awareness, the greatest joy you can feel is knowing that you are giving to a worthy cause. Working in the community requires individuals to understand their relationship with the community and the way that leadership generally emerges in the community context.

Every leader is also a member of a community — with the community contributing to the development of the leader's personal identity. Leaders who have a strong personal identification with a community based on pride of membership also usually have a strong desire to help improve the community. At the same time, true leadership in the community is informal and based on the members of the community recognizing that an individual has the abilities and vision necessary to improve the community. From this perspective, working in the community involves some leadership qualities that are similar to other contexts. Working in the community requires establishing a vision for the future that will benefit the community and influencing the other members of the community to adopt the vision as their own. Working in the community differs from leadership in other contexts because it often involves shared or rotating leadership, with the leader functioning as a servant of the community interests.

In general, the dynamics of working in the community require leaders to distinguish between their personal interests and the needs of the community (Alexander 2011). While personal interests can include the opportunity for tangible gain, they can also include the desire to gain status or importance as a leader in the community. Working in the community requires leaders to set aside their personal interests and focus on the interests and needs of the community as defined by the members of the community.

Systems theory suggests that all human organizations, including communities, are similar to biological organisms and require energy inputs and care to thrive (Parada and Homan 2011). The system takes in energy from the external environment to grow and to maintain stability. It accomplishes this through transactions with other systems, such as commercial trading with other communities or interactions with larger political units. When an event occurs to create an imbalance in the community, the system must adjust to restore balance and to ensure that the community can continue to thrive.

Dynamics of the Community

A community can be viewed as a series of interrelated subsystems that interact to form a network that represents the social structure of the community system. The community operates by cooperation among the various subsystems in the network. It also operates to some degree by consensus, although full consensus is not essential for communities to function smoothly. Some of the various subsystems interacting in a community are political, educational, health, and religious.

Because the subsystems in the community are interrelated, changes in one subsystem will generally result in changes to all subsystems — which represent the fundamental dynamic of a community. From this perspective, a community can be considered a complex adaptive system composed of numerous subsystems interacting with each other based on rules established by the community (O'Grady and Malloch 2010). This type of system consists of numerous networks that are interconnected to such a degree that a change to one subsystem requires other subsystems to adjust. The community system is adaptive, because it can change over time in response to changes in the external environment. In effect, the community system can adapt to the environment by making changes in the way individual subsystems operate and relate to each other. This process is analogous to the way organisms change in response to environmental changes (Buckley 1998).

The view of the community as a complex adaptive system assumes that the various subsystems within the community function with relative equality. For example, the educational subsystem and the health subsystem have similar importance to the operation of the community over the long run. The response to a change in the environment, however, can lead to a temporary increase in the importance of a subsystem, but the relationships between the networks will return to equilibrium after the community adapts. For example, the community can emphasize the health subsystem after the outbreak of an illness, but after the community adapts by treating the illness, the relationships among the subsystems return to an equilibrium state. This model suggests that the traditional view of the relationships among subsystems as a hierarchical model in which the political network exerts full control over the community is not viable. The subsystems and their networked interrelationships allow the community to adapt to changes in the environment— regardless of the degree of control that a single subsystem attempts to exert over the community (O'Grady and Malloch 2010).

The behavior of individuals, subsystems, and networks in the complex adaptive system of the community is fundamentally unpredictable. The inability to accurately forecast outcomes is because the community network and subsystems have many agents placing pressure on the community and many individual actors continuously working together to respond to changes in the external environment. These various actors can be viewed as independent variables that cannot be measured or analyzed to predict their course of action. While historical responses of the community to similar situations can provide some insight about the way a community is likely to respond to an environmental change, the actual response remains uncertain because of the large number of variables affecting the operation of the individual subsystems and the community as a whole.

A particular characteristic of complex adaptive systems is emergence, which refers to the way that seemingly random interactions among agents lead to new system configurations to adapt to the environment. The system reorganizes itself as required to survive or to thrive in the changed environment. The process is dynamic, because it receives input from many sources and agents with the possibility that the rules controlling interactions among subsystems will change. In addition, the emergent dynamic theoretically allows the subsystem to respond as soon as the need for change becomes apparent, creating a proactive element to process. The end result is a community that is better able to respond to the changes in the environment and develop approaches to allow it to continue to prosper and thrive.

Working in the Community System

Working in the community system is a variant of team leadership, with each community network or subsystem functioning as a team. It requires assessing the stage of development of the subsystem based on the stages of team development as discussed in chapter 7. It also requires understanding the relationships among the actors in the various subsystems in the community. Many individuals in the community participate in multiple subsystems and produce a network effect—leading to interrelationships among subsystems.

The community subsystems generally have both formal and informal leaders, with the informal leader often acting as the change agent when adaptive change is necessary. While the formal leader has certain assigned tasks, the informal leader adopts the roles that the leader does not fulfill. Informal leaders can be considered emergent leaders in the community, because they appear or emerge when there is a need for leadership that is not met by the existing formal leader. In many situations, emergent leaders have more influence in the subsystem than the formal leader.

In the community environment characterized by the interaction of many different subsystems, an effective leader exerts influence on the networks of subsystems rather than on a single or individual subsystem. For example, an individual who participates in the education subsystem may become an informal leader based on others recognizing his or her superior knowledge about a topic. To be effective in producing change in the community, however, this informal leader has to force relationships with the leaders in the other community subsystems that comprise the community network. Both the formal and informal leaders of community subsystems function as nodes connecting the subsystems, which allows the community to function as an integrated whole. An effective leader in the community setting influences the community network by influencing the leaders of the subsystems. The leaders of the subsystems then interact with each other to influence the larger community network formed by the subsystems.

An additional consideration when working in the complex adaptive system of the community is the need for a leader to maintain balance between the external forces and internal forces pressuring the community. The external environment creates the need for the community to change.

These external forces can be financial, social, political, or religious. The external forces are also a source of the energy to maintain the community that is created from the transactions between the community and other organizations. The internal forces resist change because of the uncertainty as to the outcome of the change process. These forces can include available resources, roles of individuals within the community, and the configuration and structure of community institutions. The role of the leader is to adopt a strategic and predictive orientation, assessing how the external forces will affect the community and the way in which the community should adapt to the external forces. The leader then attempts to influence the subsystems to take the steps necessary to make the adaptations. Some of the possible steps include reconfiguration of the subsystems to produce changes in the larger community system, increasing or improving the skills of the individuals in a subsystem, and improving integration or cooperation among subsystems.

Considerations When Working in the Community

A particularly important consideration when working in the community is to ensure that your motives and actions demonstrate a genuine desire to benefit the community. Individuals in the community, including the formal and informal leaders of various subsystems, respond when they believe that the efforts of others will promote the well-being of the community. This includes the perception that the efforts of others will advance the interests of the subsystem equitably. To a large degree, this consideration is similar to the need for you to demonstrate the sincerity and authenticity that are derived from passion to influence others effectively.

When working in the community, it is necessary to ensure that a benefit to one subsystem in the community does not produce a detriment to another subsystem in the community (Parada and Homan 2011). Because of the interconnectivity of the various subsystems in the community network, any harm caused to one subsystem can have an effect on many other subsystems. Members of the community are less likely to trust your motive and judgment if actions you take benefit some at the expense of others. Working in the community should also involve techniques intended to bring people together to make joint decisions. A particularly important skill necessary to bring people together in the community is the ability to rapidly synthesize large amounts of data to identify the underlying issues in a situation. It is also important to establish a network of personal relationships with individuals in some of the many community subsystems. These relationships act as both a source of information and a means of exerting influence on the community. It is important to be able to develop a strategic imperative for the community that others perceive as relevant and necessary.

It is almost seven years since David decided to be active in his neighborhood. Since then he pushed to have laws in place to preserve his neighborhood. His neighbors trust him and realize that he is not just passionate about the neighborhood but also about protecting the people. He still works at his job in Manhattan, and his parents are proud and happy he has this passion.

Summary

Working in the community requires an understanding of the dynamics affecting the interrelationships of the community subsystems and the way leadership emerges.

The community is composed of many subsystems dedicated to community needs — such as education or health — with the interaction of the subsystems creating a community network. The network balances inputs and outputs to meet the needs of the community. The community can be viewed as a complex adaptive system, because it responds to changes in the external environment that produce an imbalance in the network by changing the operation of one or more subsystems. Because of the network connections, a change in one subsystem produces changes in other subsystems. This type of system is characterized by emergence, which involves self-reorganization to maintain balance or equilibrium. During this process, informal leaders emerge as necessary to guide the community through changes. Working in the community requires ensuring that the community members perceive that motives and actions will benefit the community. It also requires ensuring that a change intended to benefit one subsystem will not harm another subsystem.

Case Study 8: A Community in Trouble

A small community in a rural area between two major cities has been experiencing difficulties with its schools that include problems with retaining teachers and poor attendance rates. The head of the school system in the community has asked Jemma, a specialist in education administration, for help in determining the cause of the schools' problems and what can be done to fix them. Jemma has lived in the city all her life and has been successful in helping large urban schools identify problems and make improvements. Jemma's plan for investigating the issues was to first examine the school records and then talk with teachers, students, and parents to gather more information.

The examination of the school records was not very helpful and only showed the extent of the problem of teachers leaving the school and the poor attendance rate. Although she wants to gather more information from people involved with the school system, she is treated as an outsider. Nonetheless, she has learned that some of the teachers have left their positions because they believed living in a city would provide them with more social and financial opportunities. She also found that some of the absences were because of the need for children to care for elderly grandparents or to help with family work. While she has the support of the head of the school system, some of the other individuals in the community are concerned that any changes to the schools could be costly to the community.

Questions:

1. What are some of the subsystems in this community, and how do they interact?
2. How can Jemma improve her ability to work in this community?
3. What recommendation would you make to retain teachers in the community?
4. What recommendation would you make to improve school attendance among children in the community?

References

Alexander, N. 2012. *Guide to Understanding Leadership*. Florida

Bass, B., and R. Bass. 2008. *The Bass Handbook of Leadership*. New York, NY: Free Press.

Buckley, W. 1998. *Society: A Complex Adaptive System*. Amsterdam, Netherlands: OPA.

www.ingramcontent.com/pod-product-compliance
Lightning Source LLC
Chambersburg PA
CBHW070837180526
45168CB00002B/857